MW00534902

The Beatles in Rishikesh

Paul Saltzman
Foreword by Stephen Maycock
Viking Studio

The Beatles in Rishikesh

ACKNOWLEDGMENTS

I'd like to thank Lewis Lapham, Farley Mowat, and Barbara Turner for their writing inspiration. Stephen Maycock honored this book with his foreword. I thank him for his encouragement when he first saw these photos at Sotheby's in London, and Brad Lemee, whose desire to add these photos to his collection led me to Stephen.
My sincere thanks to Michelle Lefolii for her excellent and detailed research, to Simone Lefolii and JoAnne Gestrin for additional research and office assistance, and to Vijay and Kiran Dhar and Rupa Lal for their openhearted hospitality. And finally, I'd like to express my heartfelt appreciation to Patricia Aquino for our love without strings, and for her overall help with research, computer problem solving both at home and in India, first stage proofreading, and overall joyful times.

VIKING STUDIO

Published by the Penguin Group
Penguin Putnam Inc., 375 Hudson Street, New York, New York 10014, U.S.A.Penguin Books Ltd, 27 Wrights Lane, London W8 5TZ, England***Penguin Books Australia Ltd, Ringwood, Victoria, Australia***Penguin Books Canada Ltd, 10 Alcorn Avenue, Toronto, Ontario, Canada M4V 3B2***Penguin Books (N.Z.) Ltd, 182-190 Wairau Road, Auckland 10, New Zealand***Penguin Books Ltd, Registered Offices: Harmondsworth, Middlesex, England***First published in 2000 by Viking Studio, a member of Penguin Putnam Inc.

1 3 5 7 9 10 8 6 4 2

John and Paul

CIP data available ***ISBN 0-670-89261-0

Printed in China ***Set in HTF Mazarin***DESIGNER: Tom Brown (TBA+D) ***ASSISTANT DESIGNER: Jenn Roberts ***Without limiting the rights under copyright reserved above, no part of this publication may be reproduced, stored in or introduced into a retrieval system, or transmitted, in any form or by any means (electronic, mechanical, photocopying, recording or otherwise), without the prior written permission of both the copyright owner and the above publisher of this book.

During the years 1963-1970, the Beatles were undoubtedly among the most photographed subjects in the world. After Beatlemania had taken hold, first in Britain and then in the United States, the Fab Four's every move both as a group and as individuals was captured on film and reported in the media. At first, flush with unimagined fame and fortune, they were seemingly happy to play to the cameras. We now know that the grueling schedule of touring and the glare of constant publicity turned the dream into a near nightmare, particularly for John and George. George it was who, on August 29, 1966, after what turned out to be their final official concert, at Candlestick Park in San Francisco, announced to the others that he would rather leave the group than continue to go through the motions of performing for thousands of screaming fans. Neither the fans nor the Beatles themselves could hear what was being played, and the whole business of live appearances had become thoroughly irksome. *** Having made the decision to stop touring, and feeling, no doubt, a great weight lifted from their shoulders, the Beatles then spent the next few months focusing their attention on individual projects. Paul turned his hand to writing the score for the film *The Family Way*, John went off to shoot *How I Won the War* in Germany and Spain, and George flew to Bombay to further his increasingly serious interest in Indian music and philosophy. It was through him that the other Beatles were introduced to Transcendental Meditation and the Maharishi Mahesh Yogi. In February 1968, the Beatles traveled to the Maharishi's Academy in Rishikesh, India. Although a private event, the Beatles' visit was recorded in limited newsreel footage together with photographs taken by a few individuals at the academy who, like Paul Saltzman, suddenly found themselves rubbing shoulders with arguably the most famous men of the period—this at a time when opportunities for photographing two or more of the group together were increasingly rare. In more than a decade of dealing with Beatles memorabilia, I have been privileged to see many of these photographs. *** Several years ago, Paul Saltzman arrived in my office, inquisitive as to whether his pictures would be of interest to collectors.

With the two of us hunched over a light box, he laid out transparencies that had remained essentially unseen for nearly thirty years and I well remember the impact those images had. It was difficult to believe they had been taken so long ago: the colors were so vibrant and the overall quality was such that I was surprised to learn that Paul was not a professional. Some of the shots are the best I have seen, not only of this particular event, but of the many informally taken pictures of the group through the 1960s that have surfaced over the years. ✳✳✳ Looking at them again, I find the most striking images to be those of John Lennon and Paul McCartney with their guitars. Sunburned and unshaven, they look relaxed and happy, quite at ease in front of Paul Saltzman's camera. These pictures would seem to contradict the generally held idea that they had all but given up on collaboration in their songwriting by this date. The intimacy of these frames is quite remarkable and the photos perfectly capture perhaps the most positive aspect of this Indian interlude: a newfound burst of creativity. In these few months, away from distractions and commitments back home, John, Paul, and George composed most of the songs for what would be the next album, entitled simply *The Beatles* but universally known as the White Album, eventually released in November of that year. ✳✳✳ Ultimately, these portraits of John and Paul have a poignancy, recording as they do a partnership that was to be pulled apart by the tensions that crystallized in the months following the Beatles' return to England. Despite the steadily disintegrating relationships within the group, the Beatles still managed to record three albums and continued to have number-one hits. Finally, almost two years exactly after the Indian trip, on April 10, 1970, Paul McCartney announced that the group had officially split up. ✳✳✳ The publication of Paul Saltzman's photographs is to be welcomed by both fans and historians of the Beatles alike, for these images provide a significant addition to the detail of what is a relatively little-recorded episode in the career of the most important rock group the world has known.

—*Stephen Maycock*

In the mid-1960s, with drugs, sex, and rock and roll, shifting family values, and the Vietnam War heating up, our generation turned up the volume. Everything was up for reevaluation, including one's own psyche, and I jumped in, headfirst. I'd already graduated from high school, playing sports and getting mediocre marks, flunked out of engineering after four years of university, and driven south to Mississippi, joining the Student Nonviolent Coordinating Committee (SNCC). In the summer of 1965, I helped blacks register for the vote, was jailed for ten days along with many other civil rights workers, and was punched in the face by Byron De La Beckwith Jr., KKK member and son of Byron De La Beckwith Sr. (played by James Woods in the film *Ghosts of Mississippi*). The younger Beckwith got off scot-free when a racist judge believed his four friends who witnessed the assault and testified they hadn't seen a thing. I had also worked in front of and behind the cameras in public affairs television for the Canadian Broadcasting Corporation, worked at the National Film Board of Canada, smoked dope, done psychedelics, loved the Beatles, gotten laid, given out flowers to motorists in rush hour on Yonge Street, Toronto's main drag, and loved the life I was living. ***But deep down I lacked a sense of peace, of self-confidence, even a sense of meaning for my life. Late in 1967, I stuffed my backpack with clothes, chocolate bars, notebooks, and a stainless-steel water bottle and set out on a journey to "find myself." The only country that attracted me was India, so that's where I headed. ***I said good-bye to my girlfriend and arranged to end my time at the National Film Board with one last job. If I could get myself to India, I'd be

Temple by the Ganges, Haridwar

hired as a local soundman on a three-person documentary film shoot. The NFB director I'd be working with asked if I had done sound before. Without missing a beat I said absolutely and then rushed to a sound recordist I knew and said, "Teach me, please!" *** On December 4, 1967, with two hundred dollars and a round-trip ticket to New Delhi in my pocket, and the new skill of film sound recording in hand, I boarded a plane for my first trip abroad. *** India was mind-blowing. I did well on the film shoot, and met the Beatles at the Maharishi Mahesh Yogi's ashram in Rishikesh, where I took some pictures of them. When I eventually returned home to Toronto, I wrote a short magazine article and published a few of my photos. I then put them away in a cardboard box, and forgot about them. *** Thirty years later, my daughter, Devyani, fell in love with the Beatles' music. One afternoon late

Lakshman Jhoola, Rishikesh

in 1998, she walked into my study while I was E-mailing and asked, "Dad, didn't you once tell me that you met the Beatles in India in the sixties and took some pictures of them?" I told her I had and she said she would love to see them.

This book is the result of Devyani's enthusiasm and encouragement after seeing the photos, and of the excitement and support of my New York literary agent and friend, Joe Regal. It is also the result of the enthusiasm of Christopher Sweet at Viking Studio, and the beautiful design work of Tom Brown. *** I am delighted with the opportunity this book has given me to recall my long-ago journey to India, a time of profound personal change, and my encounter with the Beatles, and to revisit Rishikesh itself earlier this year. And, not least, to share with you these photographs and the anecdotes that unfolded with them.

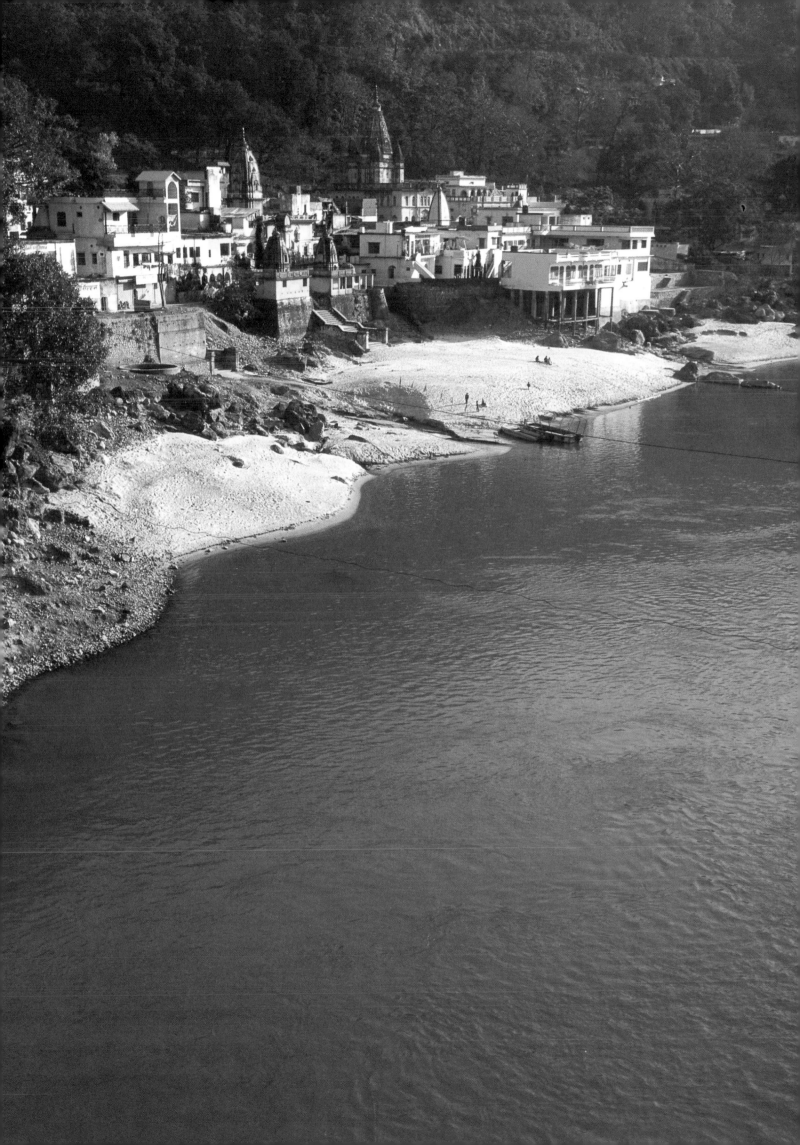

As I look out the window of Emirates Air Flight 733, coming in to land in New Delhi, a wide smile spreads across my face. I feel a sense of joy welling up. It spreads from the center of my heart, until my whole chest is warm and softly vibrating. It's like I'm coming home. I remember I had felt something similar when I first came to India. *** It was December 6, 1967. I was twenty-three then, and I felt the wonderful winter heat of Bombay bathe my body. My neck and back stretched out and stood tall, and my shoulders came upright from their long-defensive hunch. My chest opened up, feeling unrestricted, and my breathing became deep and relaxed, like I couldn't remember. I loved India, that first week, just for that. Just for the visceral, joyful feeling of coming home to a place within myself that I had long forgotten. *** I went to India to get away from the world I had grown up in. To change myself. I wasn't at ease within myself. I always had to be around other people so I wouldn't have to be alone with me. *** That first trip changed my life. It was my first conscious step on the journey within, which George Harrison wrote about so beautifully in his songs "Within You, Without You" and "The Inner Light." It would be only a few weeks later and a few city blocks from where I was staying that George would first record "The Inner Light"—on January 12, 1968, at EMI's studios in Bombay—and I couldn't have imagined that by mid-February of that year my path would unexpectedly cross his, and that of the other Beatles, in Rishikesh. *** It's still dark outside as the car drops me at the New Delhi train station to take the 7:10 A.M. Shatabdi Express north to Haridwar en route to revisit the Maharishi's ashram. It's a journey of pleasure. I've been in India many times since 1968, visiting family, making films, traveling, exploring. But this is my first visit back—almost thirty-two years to the day—to the place where I learned meditation. ***As we pull out of the train station, laborers in soiled clothes unloading baskets of bananas and cashew nuts on the next platform, we slowly move through the city, waking up to a warm sunrise, pink light bathing the houses and roadways in a soft morning glow. Soon, one- and two-story houses and factories give way to open fields, where several men squat for a morning pee. Picking up speed as we skim across the vast open plains that lead north and east to the foothills of the Himalayas, the countryside turning yellow in the morning sunlight, we see field after field cultivated with vegetables, grains, and sugarcane, their two-foot-long green leaves fanning out like moptop haircuts on slender seven-foot stalks. ***We zip over bridges, crossing arrow-straight irrigation canals and past small villages that dot the landscape. In the small city of Roorkee a primary school has set its red plastic chairs outside, in neat clumps of twenty to twenty-five, each class studying about ten feet from the next. I love how India lives out-of-doors. We speed by rows of tall eucalyptus trees, through lush banana groves, and past fields semi-submerged in irrigation waters, glistening in the now bright sunlight. Flocks of white herons glide from field to field eating seeds and bugs as the many shades of green dance before my eyes. As a tiny, quaint village of squat, whitewashed houses rushes past, children are flying richly colored saffron, white, and green kites in a field near the tracks. It's good to be back. India was mind-blowing thirty years ago. It is mind-blowing now. ***The alluvial plains end suddenly as the foothills, cloaked in deciduous trees, announce the start of the Himalayas and our train slows into the station at

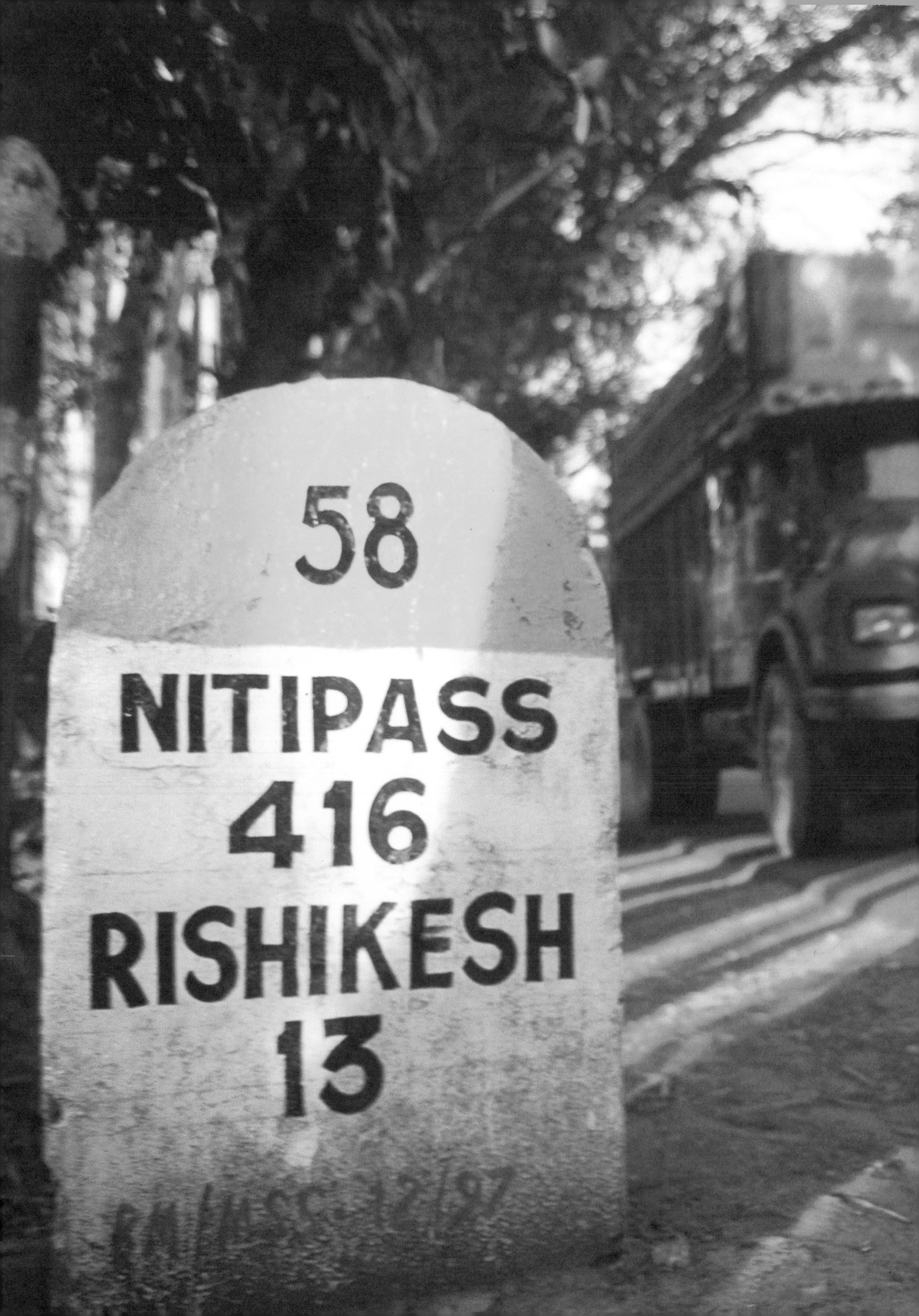
58
NITIPASS
416
RISHIKESH
13

20

Haridwar. A medium-size town, Haridwar sits on the Ganges River and serves as a rail gateway to Rishikesh. As I step onto the platform a porter is immediately by my side, reaching for my bag.

PREVIOUS PAGES: On the road to Rishikesh

"Porter, sahib?" he asks in a professional but keen tone. He's dressed in traditional porter's clothes—a long-used, faded burgundy-colored turban around his head; a slightly tattered, loose, almost matching cotton top hangs open from his shoulders; an old dirt-brown cotton lungi is wrapped around his waist, pulled up in front and tucked in so he can move quickly—and he has the official railway porter's curved brass medallion tied around his upper left bicep. He's weathered, strong, about forty-five years old, with the kind of noble face you'd see on a soldier painted in an old Indian miniature. He hoists my overnight bag onto his head and strides off toward the taxi stand outside. I grab my backpack, sling it over one shoulder, and move to stay with him. *** We reach the cab stand, just outside the front gates of the station, and are immediately approached by half a dozen drivers, all wanting my fare. Choosing a white Ambassador taxicab, I negotiate with the driver and we settle on 350 rupees, or just over eight dollars, for the forty-minute ride to Rishikesh. *** Twenty-four kilometers up the road, at 1175 feet above sea level, we enter Rishikesh. The majesty of the Himalayas begins as the Shivalik range towers another 5500 feet above the town that straddles the banks of the Ganges. To India's eight hundred million Hindus, the Ganges is Ganga Ma—or Mother Ganges—the holiest of rivers, making Rishikesh a pilgrimage center filled with temples and hostels. A center for yoga, meditation, and philosophical studies since ancient times, it also has many ashrams, both in the town and in the hills around, like the Maharishi

Mahesh Yogi's, the object of my return. In a surprising change from when I was last here, tourist brochures now also advertise twelve trekking and river-rafting companies. *** According to Hindu mythology, Mother Ganga, said to be the daughter of the Lord of the Himalayas, originated in the celestial realms. It flowed from the lotuslike foot of the god Vishnu, the preserver of all life in the Hindu trinity of supreme beings, eventually cascading to earth; its torrential fall from the heavens broken by Shiva, the destroyer in the trinity, who let it flow through his hair until it gently brought life to the earth. The goddess Ganga is said to give life and fertility to those who bathe in her waters, to purify all sins, and to give eternal life to those who die by her banks and whose ashes are set upon her waters. In this earthly realm, the Ganges begins its journey from the Gangotri glacier, from a cave called Gaumukh, meaning "mouth of the cow," 70 miles northeast of Rishikesh, and more than 10,000 feet up in the Himalayas. From there it flows 1560 miles to Calcutta and beyond into the Bay of Bengal and the Indian Ocean.

The next morning, I hire a car, driver, and guide to cover as much ground as possible over the next two days. No one, including Rama, my guide, knows of the Beatles and their visit here in 1968, even after I show numerous photographs. *** Pulling into the parking area near the central ghat, or steps to the river, we head down a short street full of tourist shops I don't recall being here in 1968. As we turn a corner of the narrow walkway that leads between two low buildings to the ghat, we approach five middle-aged men sitting against a wall, some with a hand outstretched, asking for money. While they are not traditional sadhus, dressed in saffron-orange clothes and who eat

through the kindness of others, they seem in need and are both friendly and undemanding. This is how they support themselves, and drawn by their fascinating faces, I stop. They are good-humored, even playful, and before walking to the boats, I donate some rupees to their expenses. As will happen in Rishikesh when I pass them or others I've given to again, they will not ask a second time. Unless, of course, it's the next business day. * * * In contrast to 1968, now only large, powerful, multi-colored outboard motorboats are used to ferry as many as thirty-five to forty people on each crossing. The monsoon rains that bring the silt runoff down from the Himalayas are still months away, and the Ganges is a clear blue-green color. The return trip from the Triveni ghat costs fifteen cents each, and as we near the far shore, the main spiritual area of Rishikesh called Swargashram, another ghat extends almost the whole half-mile-long frontage of ashrams and temples. As we alight and go up the steps, a marvelous, brightly painted, saffron and red face watches us approach.

PRECEDING PAGES: Lakshman Jhoola Bridge; Three beggars; OPPOSITE: A man dressed as the god Hanuman

It seems, since his patient eye contact is only with me, that he sees more rupees forthcoming from foreigners than from native pilgrims. He's dressed impeccably, head to foot, as the Hindu god Hanuman, the monkey god, complete with a long tail curved up behind his back. Hanuman is, among other things, a symbol of health, and our human Hanuman is most pleasant as he offers in halting English to perform his god's ritual dance for Rama and me. I decline, keen to get to the ashram.

We head south, down one of only two short narrow streets on the east side of the river, passing ashrams, temples, shops, and restaurants before leaving town and walking along a sandy path

27

angling toward the river's edge. I can't locate the dirt path that led me up the cliff to the Maharishi's ashram thirty-two years before, and while Rama knows of the ashram, he has never been to it. Where I remember the path being, there now sits a small three-room dwelling. No one is home, but after a few minutes an old sadhu returns. When I explain my purpose, he laughs heartily and says that thirty-two years is a long time. He explains that a major flood poured down the river valley in 1976, so momentous that as it banked this bend in the Ganges, it rose almost to the top of the two-hundred-foot high cliff. In the process, it washed away houses, flooded much of Rishikesh, and took with it the path. He points a hundred yards back the way we came and says we'll find the way there. He has such a lovely countenance that I ask if I may take his picture. He says yes, and as we talk he shows a wonderfully youthful energy, and he doesn't miss a thing. ***His name is Narayan Swami and he surprises me with his age, eighty-five. When asked, he explains that "swami" is a title of respect bestowed upon a teacher by his followers. He spends his days in meditation and teaching; eats one vegetarian meal a day, at noon; and studies the Hindu holy texts extensively. He was married when he was twelve and his bride was eight. He was a poor farmer in Bihar, and when his wife died at thirty-seven he continued farming until his three sons and daughter were all married. ***"There were no problems at home and I had finished all my family responsibilities," he says, and wanting to attain peace, he left on a path of self-realization. He is very happy, having been a sadhu and now a swami these past forty-two years. He sees his children often and they are, he adds, "very pleased with the life I am living." ***He was here in 1968 but doesn't know about the Beatles, or any of the rest of us who were here, because he was in solitude and meditation. ✳✳✳ Rama and I round the corner where Narayan Swami had pointed and walk up a gently sloping gravelway leading away from the Ganges. A hundred yards from the river, we come to a huge gray stone gate to the ashram, standing almost twenty feet high and comprised of three archways, each topped by a domed roof. It's a long way from the simple, white picket fence gate that George, John, Paul, Ringo, and the rest of us had entered. We pass beneath its domes and climb the steep driveway that leads to a guardhouse and an eight-foot-high, hunter-green wrought-iron set of gates. ✳✳✳ Finding no one there, we enter. The guard is resting a short distance away and, seeing us, rushes over with a surprised and worried look. Rama translates for me that no one is allowed in without permission and that foreigners are not allowed. A month earlier I'd called numerous times to the head office of the Maharishi's organization in Holland, where he now lives, to see if permission was needed, and although return calls had been promised, none came. Rama ascertains that no one in authority will be back today, and we decide to return the next day. ✳✳✳ Early the next morning, as we take another boat across, an ethereal, wispy morning mist rises from the river, all around us, and for a moment I think of the River Styx. We arrive at the ashram midmorning. This time two guards call a Mr. Thakkar to come to the front gates. A slight man of about forty-five, with fine-boned features, he's dressed in a light gray cotton shirt and an off-white cotton lungi. He's friendly when he hears my request to revisit and to do a short meditation in the ashram. Smiling knowingly when I tell him that learning meditation here in 1968 changed my life, he graciously invites us into the reception area for a glass of water and arranges for a guide to show

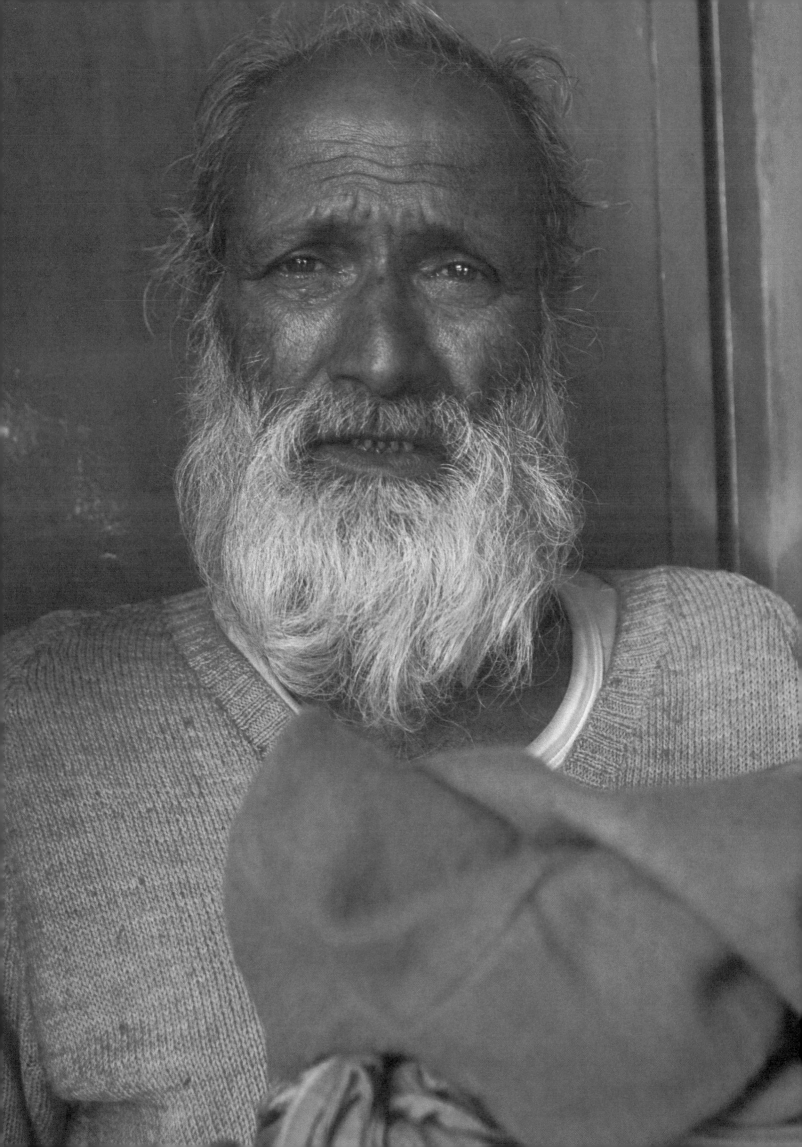

us the grounds, with the instruction that we are to be left alone while I meditate. *** We walk a roadway parallel to the river from the reception building toward the wooded hills beyond the ashram's south end. It's immediately clear that almost everything has changed. The grounds are at least five times more expansive and, as yet, I can't see one building still standing from 1968. We walk beneath the many lovely trees, stepping in and out of warm pools of bright January sun. The whitewashed, simple, flat-roofed bungalows have all been replaced with large, fancy, two- and three-story apartment buildings for those attending meditation courses. The increased fortunes of the Maharishi's organization are clearly seen in the transformation of the ashram. I am reminded of Mal Evans first telling me, back in 1968, near where we are now walking, of the Beatles' concern with the Maharishi's inordinate attention to money. *** As we continue through the new ashram, I feel a deep sense of pleasure not only returning to this place of past personal transformation, but also for the ripple effect it has had through my life since then. Walking around, I find that it's impossible to tell exactly where events had taken place back then. There are many new buildings, staff quarters, and an extensive area of individual meditation cells, each a small two-story stone building, matching the

Narain Swami; FOLLOWING PAGES:
Crossing the Ganges

ashram's arched stone gateway. On this day, the ashram is empty except for several staff, their families, and two older sadhus, one brushing his teeth as we pass by, the other washing his clothes. I recognize only two buildings from the past—the large lecture hall and the Maharishi's bungalow. We turn right and head toward the cliff overlooking the river. Several families of large, silver-gray, long-tailed langur monkeys, their faces black and wary,

31

ke a footprint left in
he sand, and I'm reminded
f the path that's been
washed away and the
Buddhist proverb, "You
an never enter the same
iver twice." As the ashram
knew is gone, so too are
he Beatles. And yet,
e can evoke their magic
hrough their music,
heir words, and their
hotographs

35

see us approach and scamper away when we get too close. At the edge of the cliff, I recognize the area where I had first met John, George, Paul, and Ringo. Now only rough wild grass, it had been the location of the shaded long table where they and the other famous folks hung out and where I occasionally joined them. By now, our guide has left us on our own, and I sit down cross-legged with my back against a small tree, a foot from the cliff's edge. ✳✳✳ Looking over the edge of the cliff, its steep, brown earth falling away to the blue-gray boulders along the banks of the Ganges far below, I watch the wide river burble and dance through two wide bends as it traces the edge of Rishikesh. As my body takes a deep, slow breath, again I feel joy surfacing from within, like iridescent silver bubbles rising through a calm Algonquin lake at sunset. It was so right to return here. I close my eyes and listen to the sounds of the river and the soft wind purring in the trees. Dropping inside, meditating, I feel a profound calm and internal harmony. ✳✳✳ After some time, slowly coming out of the meditation, I hear a rustling and open my eyes to see a baby monkey climbing in the bushes, looking for food. Rama sits nearby. As we get up to leave I notice a single old rubber sandal in the underbrush, like a footprint left in the sand, and I'm reminded of the path that's been washed away and the Buddhist proverb, "You can never enter the same river twice." As the ashram I knew is gone, so too are the Beatles. And yet, we can evoke their magic through their music, their words, and their photographs, making that time in Rishikesh in 1968 tangible again—if but for a moment.

ON THE WAY TO RISHIKESH, 1968

Landing in the early dawn's dust and heat of Bombay on December 6, 1967, I was four days shy of my twenty-fourth birthday and I'd never been out of North America. Culture shock hit hard. I spent the first three nights in a Salvation Army hostel, for a dollar fifty a night including three meals and tea. The first night, my two hundred dollars in U.S. traveler's checks were stolen and I was awakened at 5:30 the next morning by an earthquake. Nonetheless, I was amazed by India, by its richness and its poverty. The streets around the hostel stank of sewage and yet the clothes, the music, the art, and the smell of the incense were exquisite. *** And the people were remarkably hospitable. If I looked lost on a street corner for thirty seconds someone immediately came up to offer directions. Often, they were very curious and asked questions. "What is your name?" "Where are you from?" "Are you married?" "How do you like India?" And several times I was invited into their homes for tea and conversation. *** When the NFB director and his cameraman arrived a few days later, I moved across the road into the Taj Mahal Hotel. The premier luxury hotel in Bombay, it was renowned for its ornate British raj architecture. I was now living in luxury on the film production's budget. After two days, we drove north by Econoline van, filming up the beautiful west coast of Gujarat and across the western scrub lands of Rajasthan. At a dusty intersection of two dirt roads in the middle of nowhere, without a structure in sight, we saw two small wooden signs nailed haphazardly to a stubby pole. Pointing north, one announced KANDLA & BEYOND; the other pointed east and read KOTA, ETC. *** We finished our filming, and on January 24, 1968, we drove into New Delhi. A letter from my girlfriend back home was waiting for me. She had moved in with someone else, and as I read her "Dear Paul" letter that first night in Delhi, my heart felt smashed by a sledgehammer. I could hear a screaming inside me that I

37

feared if I let it out I would drown in it. I could barely breathe through the tears. I felt totally abandoned, alone. ✳✳✳ Trouble too, I was now off the production budget, nearly broke, and had to check out of the Oberoi

PRECEDING PAGES: A temple by the Ganges, Swargashram

Intercontinental Hotel the next day. Fortunately, two guardian angels appeared. Jim George, Canadian high commissioner for India, and his wife, Carol, invited me to crash at their palatial official residence at number 4 Aurangzeb Road. ✳✳✳ After I checked out of the Oberoi, I walked into the hot midafternoon sun and found a crowd of between thirty and forty press people milling about. Even though I'd worked in current affairs television for several years, I had never experienced a news scrum. A gaggle of journalists, reporters, news photographers, cameramen, and soundmen were camped outside waiting for someone to arrive. A moment later, a white chauffeur-driven Ambassador, then the most common car in India, pulled in and at a shout they all grabbed their news gear. Paparazzi-like, they swarmed the car. The object of the hunt, a petite, wispy, beautiful young woman, could barely get herself out of the car. As she and her female friend were rushed into the lobby by hotel staff, the press crushed around yelling out questions, microphones thrust forward, cameras rolling, snapping photographs. I recognized Mia Farrow from the numerous pictures I'd seen of her in newsmagazines some months earlier, when her marriage to Frank Sinatra had ended. ✳✳✳ Mia was clearly shaken and frightened by the rapaciousness of the newspeople as they all pushed past me in pursuit of her. Two large Sikh doormen, wearing starched white uniforms and crimson-red turbans, blocked the press from entering as three assistant managers rushed Mia and her friend through the

40

lobby toward a waiting elevator. One photographer slipped through a side door and as he raced up behind Mia calling her name so she'd turn around, she lost it. She ran at him, screaming, hitting him with her bag. Two security men grabbed him and ushered him out, and Mia was close to tears with a look on her face like that of a terrified child. ✻✻✻ I bought a beautiful giant yellow mum at the hotel flower shop and took the elevator up to her floor. I got off and headed down the long hall to the Maharajah Suite. The doorbell sounded quietly through the heavy mahogany double doors. After a long moment, the friend I'd seen Mia enter with opened the door. She was, I later learned, Mia's sister Prudence. I explained that I had witnessed the scene downstairs and wanted to make a kindly gesture. Prudence was wary but accepted the flower, saying she would give it to Mia, and as I turned and went back down the hall, she called after me to thank me. ✻✻✻ Winter days in New Delhi are gorgeous. Big blue skies, almost no clouds, rarely any rain, and temperatures consistently 70 to 80 degrees Fahrenheit. Taking an inexpensive yellow-and-black scooter taxi, we headed to the high commissioner's residence. I felt good. Out the open sides of the covered three-wheeler, hundreds of bicyclists and pedestrians in bright-colored saris, business suits, kurta pajamas, and a few poor beggars in rags, blurred past. As we passed the exclusive Delhi Golf Club, the putt-putt of the two-cylinder engine setting a steady musical rhythm, I understood the double-edged sword of fame in a way I never had before. ✻✻✻ As I hung around New Dehli, I was desperate for relief. A new American acquaintance, Al Bragg, asked me if I wanted to come along to hear the Maharishi Mahesh Yogi give a talk on Transcendental Meditation, and I jumped at the chance. ✻✻✻ The large auditorium at New Delhi

University was jam-packed, overflowing with foreigners and Indians as we squeezed in against the wall at the back. On stage, a low dais was festooned with flowers. After ten or fifteen minutes, a short, curious little man draped in white cotton, with long scraggly graying hair and beard, entered at the rear of the hall and walked down the center aisle. Close behind, twenty Westerners followed, each of them wearing colorful Indian clothes and garlands of red, white, and orange flowers around their necks. They were, it turned out, part of a group of meditators on their way to the Maharishi's ashram in Rishikesh. As the Maharishi sat cross-legged on the dais, his followers seated themselves in a semicircle behind him. *** The Maharishi talked in a high musical voice about meditation as a direct path to inner peace and harmony. He said, "Transcendental Meditation naturally takes the mind beyond the present level of experience to the finer stages of experience, and eventually takes it beyond the finest state of experience and leaves it in a state of pure awareness. It takes the mind behind and beyond the fears and anxieties that trouble us. Reaching those fields of pure consciousness, of pure being, we tap the very source of bliss and energy." *** All this, he said, could begin quickly and easily without conflict in the mind, and without giving up any of life's pleasures. I couldn't quite buy this. I guess I felt that the road to inner peace and happiness was one of struggle. And yet he was light and joyful, and his laughter seemed to embody what he promised was available to all of us through meditation. Standing there in the back of the auditorium, I prayed he was right. *** Several days later, I rode through the night by third-class train, north into the foothills of the Himalayas. As morning came, a dawning laven-

44

der-pink sky illuminated the forested green slopes that rose on either side of the tracks. We entered Dehra Dun, a town known for its two elite British-run private schools, its temples, and as one of two rail stops close to Rishikesh. *** An hour's ride by scooter-rickshaw took me to Rishikesh. Walking through the bustling town, past several small white temples, I arrived at the bathing steps for pilgrims that lined the river. The Ganges flowed swiftly, a dark lime green color, as I hired a small motor boat to take me across the river. The old boatman steered us out into the fast current in a wide trajectory that carried us the 150 yards to the east bank of the river. Nearing the far shore, we passed in front of the ghats on the Swargashram side of the Ganges. Men and women, young and old, were bathing and washing clothes in the bright afternoon sun. As the boatman pushed off, he pointed south along the riverbank and said, "Maharishi ashram there." *** I walked a half mile along the pebbly and rocky riverbank, until I came to a small sign pointing up a narrow path. After a circuitous and steep climb up through trees, thickets, and patches of large purple wildflowers, I reached the top of the cliff. It was early afternoon on a beautiful day. From there, a one-lane dirt road ran several hundred yards away from town, along the cliffs, leading me to the ashram. At the entrance stood a faded white wood picket gate large enough to let a small truck through. Across the road sat a one-room concrete building with a sign saying INQUIRY OFFICE. Finding no one there, I crossed back to speak to the guard standing by the gate. "Namaste," I said in Hindi, with my palms together in front of my heart, tilting my head slightly down in the traditional Indian greeting of respect. "Namaste," he said in the same manner, adding, "ashram closed." I told him I had come to learn meditation from

the Maharishi and hoped he would let me in. He told me to wait and, locking the gate behind him, walked into the ashram. He returned a few minutes later with a short young man in his early thirties, with lovely light-brown complexion and a short, dark, trim beard. He introduced himself in a quiet warm voice as Raghvendra, a disciple of the Maharishi, and asked if he could help me. I told him I had seen the Maharishi speak at Delhi University a few days before, and that I was in a lot of emotional pain. That I would like to learn meditation. Raghvendra paused long enough, it seemed, to see if I was sincere. Finally, he said, "I'm very sorry but the ashram is closed for the next several weeks for a meditation teacher's course."
I asked if I could wait or if it was possible to be taught any time sooner. He considered this for a moment, then motioned me to a straight-backed chair near the inquiry office. "I will send you tea and ask the Maharishi. But I may not be back until after dinner." ***I thanked him and dropped my backpack next to the chair, and plunked myself down. I spent the afternoon resting there and wrote a letter to my parents and one to my girl-friend, hoping she would reconsider. Before dinner Raghvendra returned. Again, he was soft-spoken and kind. *** "Maharishi says not at the present time, but perhaps soon." ***He explained that there were sixty meditators in the ashram from all over the world, to take their advanced teacher's course, and that the Beatles and their wives were there, so the ashram was closed to the press and vis-itors. I had seen three or four photographers arrive and mill around outside the gates during the course of the afternoon, until they gave up and left. ***Raghvendra added that since I had come all the way from Canada I could sleep in one of two old white canvas army tents pitched in a clearing of

scrub grass under some old teak trees near the inquiry office. He said they would also send me their simple vegetarian meals, which I could eat on the flat roof of the inquiry building. Each tent could sleep about six adults, but I was alone in mine. A local tailor from the village below had temporarily set up shop in the other tent. *** As each day stretched slowly into the next, I longed to be taught meditation. The heartache was still there. As I waited, I went for long walks, read a lot, wrote, and just looked out from my rooftop retreat. From where I sat, the many shades of yellow and green leaves of the richly colored trees dropped away into a shallow valley behind the building before swooping up the steep foothills of the Himalayas to the peaks and the pure, cerulean sky above. *** One night, despite its being the dry season in Rishikesh, it began to pour. The wind blew and the rain pelted down for twelve solid hours, soaking my tent and wetting the ground inside, but leaving me dry, for the most part.

Over the next few days Raghvendra and I talked often. A kind, decent, down-to-earth man, there was always a twinkling joy in his eyes, and whenever we looked at each other, we couldn't help smiling. Raghvendra was a *brahmacharaya*, or novice monk, and one of the Maharishi's closest disciples. He had spent many years looking for a guru and when he finally met the Maharishi, two years before, he gave up his law studies and became one of his lifetime students. *** After I'd been there for five days, an American writer came up the hill from the Ganges. Lewis Lapham had been sent from New York on assignment by the *Saturday Evening Post* to do a magazine article on the Beatles, the Maharishi, meditation, and all that was going on at the ashram. We introduced ourselves before

47

he was ushered in to see the Maharishi. He came back soon after, saying the Maharishi would give him access to the ashram but not that day. As we waited, we became friends over the next few days, spending long languid hours relaxing and laughing and talking on the flat roof of the office. Raghvendra ***Lew was a New England blue blood. His father was vice-chairman of the Bankers Trust Company and Lew was expected to become a banker like his father. But Lew had become a writer, to the chagrin of his family. "I'm the prover-bial black sheep of the family," he said one after-noon. "Writers aren't held in high esteem in New England banking circles." At night, I returned to my tent and Lew headed for a nondescript white bungalow a few yards away, where he slept, some-what uncomfortably, on an army cot.

TM

In all, I waited for just over a week. Then one day in the early morning mist, Raghvendra came through the gate and sat on the ground beside me. He told me I could come in now and learn to medi-tate. I could spend my days in the ashram, take my meals with them, and continue to sleep in the tent at night. The evening before Lewis had been granted his first interview with the Maharishi. ***My initiation into Transcendental Meditation took place in Raghvendra's quarters, with only the two of us there. We sat cross-legged on white futons on the floor and began with a short *puja*, a traditional Hindu offering of fruit, flowers, cloth, and prayers. After Raghvendra sang ancient Sanskrit prayers, he told me my mantra, or incantation, that I would use in meditating. Mantras can be words, which lose their meaning through repetition, but mine was simply a one-syllable configuration of letters that gave a soft sound when pronounced. He instructed

me in how to say the sound silently, within, and just easily follow it, listening to it until it faded to silence. And how to repeat this until I experienced a transcending of normal waking consciousness. I closed my eyes and tried it for a few minutes and Raghvendra asked me to describe what I was experi-

encing, to make sure I was using the technique properly. Then after reminding me that the mantra was mine, and secret, he left me alone to meditate for the first time. ***I relaxed, shut my eyes, and let thoughts come and go. As I became engrossed in thought the outside world seemed to recede. I no longer noticed the wind in the trees or the sound of faraway talking. Then, as Raghvendra had instructed, I gently replaced my thoughts with my mantra. I silently said my sound and listened to it, followed it. Thoughts flooded back in, and again I replaced them with my mantra. I lost sense of time, and for a moment only the sound of my mantra was in my conscious mind. As the sound faded, no verbalized thoughts replaced it, and I was left in a place without sound and without thought. I wasn't actually conscious of it until a second later, when that faithful little observation voice in my head said, "Hey! that's it!" which right away took me from that state and back into conscious verbal thought. ***I hadn't fallen asleep, yet it had been a very restful place of silence and darkness. I didn't know quite where I had gone, but I knew I had been somewhere deeply peaceful. I felt reenergized and I realized that I must have transcended. I wanted to experience it again and so continued meditating for about three-quarters of an hour and transcended once more. It could have been for a second or two, or several minutes—I couldn't tell. Most of the time, though, I just thought about things, and my thinking seemed clearer, less cluttered than usual. ***When I stopped, I waited for about a minute, slowly opened my eyes, and walked into the bright afternoon sun. It took my eyes a moment or two to adjust. I felt like a newborn chick, having just come out of its shell into a whole new reality. I walked toward my tent feeling rested, calm, mildly euphoric, turned on at being alive. As I sat on the rooftop, I couldn't help smiling at the friendly hills. I felt a soft, physical vibration in my body and a warmth in my heart. I felt a new sense of oneness with the world. The scream was gone. I realized, sitting there, that truly loving another person is not possessive or controlling but, rather, expansive and supportive. Surprisingly, I felt happiness for my girlfriend, and I realized I had abandoned her before she left me. *** That night I sat alone on the rooftop looking up at the mountain stars for hours. The trees rustled faintly in the distance, the sweet fragrance of evening jasmine filling the air. Monkeys chattered and somewhere in the valley below a lone peacock called out. From the far side of the ashram another answered. Allowing the soft, velvet touch of night to envelop me, I felt at peace. *** The ashram sat on a small plateau among wooded hills. A narrow dirt road ran from the front gate to the back of the ashram, and a barbed-wire fence surrounded the property, ensuring the ashram's privacy. Here and there along the roadway, thin, tall bamboo poles flew canary-yellow, triangular flags. Some fifteen buildings nestled in among the teak, sissoo, and guava trees. The Maharishi's bungalow sat near the cliff's edge at the front of the property, and atop its flat roof he often gave afternoon seminars for the Beatles and their group.

There was a two-story lecture hall, where the Maharishi spoke and answered questions twice a day for those on the teachers' course, and there was a kitchen building and dining hall set near the back of the ashram. Along the road away from the cliff, behind a low chainlink fence, were six long, white-washed bungalows, each with five or six double rooms. Flowerbeds filled with large red hibiscus blossoms garlanded the ashram and several vegetable gardens, tended by a turbaned old gardener, supplied some of the fresh vegetables we ate. Peacocks inhabited the surrounding woods and occasionally one would wander onto the ashram grounds.

MEET THE BEATLES

I was walking through the ashram the next morning when I saw John, Paul, George, and Ringo sitting with their partners—Cynthia Lennon, actress Jane Asher, Pattie Boyd Harrison, and Maureen Starkey—and Mal Evans at a long table by the edge of the cliff that overlooked the Ganges and Rishikesh. Somewhat nervously, I walked over. *** "May I join you?" I asked. "Sure, mate," answered John. And Paul said, "Pull up a chair." *** I sat down, and didn't know what to say. As I looked around the table, I was surprised to hear a voice yell loudly in my head, "Eeek! It's the Beatles!" Straight away, another voice inside, very calm, said, "Hey. They're just people, like you." At a pause in the conversation, John looked at me and said, "You're from the States, then?" "No, Canada," I responded. "Ah! One of the Colonies," he joked, and I said yes as we all laughed. "You're still worshipping Her Highness, then?" He was being playful and tart. Not personally, I quipped, "But we still have her on our money." "Lucky you," joked Ringo, and good-humoredly, Cynthia interceded: "Leave the chap alone, after all, he's just arrived." "No problem," I responded, and John came back with, "You see, mates, they still have a sense of humor in the Colonies!" and we laughed again. Someone got up and said they were going to meditate. Within

George Harrison

I was walking through the ashram the next morning when I saw John, Paul, George, and Ringo sitting with their partners—Cynthia Lennon, actress Jane Asher, Pattie Boyd Harrison, and Maureen Starkey—and Mal Evans at a long table by the edge of the cliff that overlooked the Ganges and Rishikesh. Somewhat nervously, walked over

OPPOSITE: The author

moments all were gone except Mal and me. I asked him if they were really as cool as they seemed. "Not always," he answered, "but pretty much." ✳✳✳ Over the following days Mal and I became buddies. He had been with the Beatles from the beginning of their success. He was a big teddy bear of a man who had been a part-time bouncer at Liverpool's Cavern Club when the Beatles played there. He was hired in 1963 by their manager, Brian Epstein, to be one of their roadies. He was a personal assistant to all four of them, taking care of their needs both in England and on the road, as he was doing in Rishikesh. He called them, "the boys." ✳✳✳ During the course of that day I asked if they minded my taking some pictures. Nobody minded at all. It was like a large easy family of meditators, and now I was included. I had my Pentax camera with 50mm and 135mm lenses, and although I had never been a photographer, I liked taking pictures. With the Beatles it was simply the fan in me.

I first became aware of the Beatles dancing to their early rock and roll songs, like "Twist and Shout," "Roll over Beethoven," and "Please, Mr. Postman." By the time "Can't Buy Me Love" hit number one on the pop charts in April 1964, I was a fan. They first toured Canada that year, and on September 7 they came to Toronto. I was then twenty-one and will never forget the feeling of electricity crackling in the air as they sang twelve songs and eighteen thousand of us, packed to the rafters in Maple Leaf Gardens, yelled and screamed and exploded so many flash bulbs that it seemed like fireworks popping all over the arena. It was a matinee performance, and after it was over we all made our way out of the Gardens into the late-afternoon summer sunlight, onto Carlton and Church streets. The police had blocked traffic from the area, and as the huge crowd of fans filled the deserted streets you could almost hear a pin drop. Electricity still tingled in the air. There was no jostling, yelling, or calling to friends; just silence parted by the odd hushed voice, everyone still transported by the magic of the Beatles. ✳✳✳ On August 8, 1966, the Beatles released their album *Revolver* in North America. I remember it vividly. Word was the album would sell out on that first day, and I speedily drove down to Sam the Record Man's big store on Yonge Street to scoop up a copy before they were all gone. Back at my house, my girlfriend and I smoked a joint, then stretched a long yellow extension cord out the front window into the warm sun and set up my hi-fi on a large multicolored Indian bedspread on the front lawn. I put the vinyl LP disc on the turntable and we lay down, cuddled up next to each other, my arm under her head, and closed our eyes. From the first note to the last I was blown away. The Beatles opened a door in my psyche. It was a key moment in my life. The song that actually did this was "Tomorrow Never Knows." Through their music, and their interviews, I had already come to trust them. I don't know any other way to say it. As I lay there on the grass, eyes closed, the sun on my face, gently stoned and superfocused, the lyrics sank into me. I knew the Beatles were telling me of a journey I had not yet made; of an internal place that held great love and knowing. ✳✳✳ The Beatles and their group ate at the table by the cliff, shaded by a flat thatched roof covered with vines and held up by white wooden poles. Breakfasts were cereal, toast, juice, tea, and coffee. Lunch and dinners were soup, plain basmati rice, and bland but nutritious vegetarian dishes with almost no spices. Sometimes I ate with them. Crows settled in the trees nearby, and monkeys gathered on the flat roof of the nearby kitchen, both waiting for an opportu-

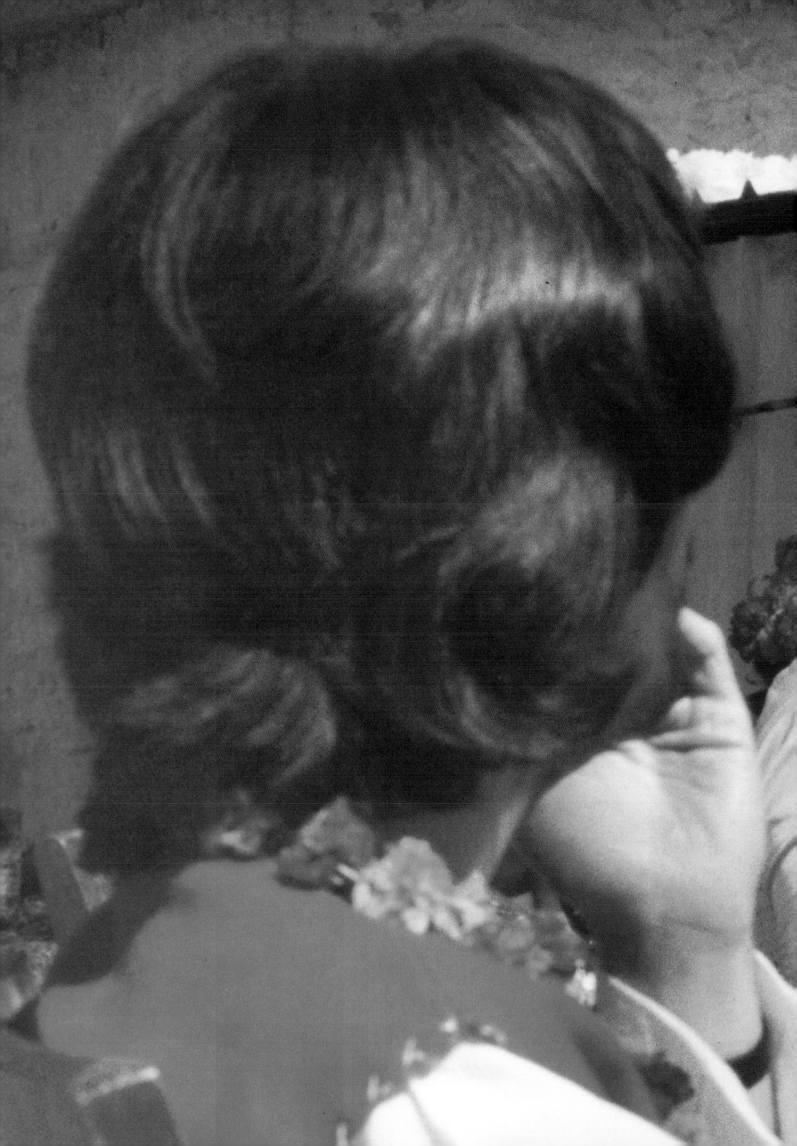

nity to grab a scrap of food someone might leave behind. Occasionally, a vulture circled lazily overhead, hanging in the updraft, pausing on its way back across the river to the nonvegetarian side of the Ganges, beyond Rishikesh. Rishikesh itself was a designated vegetarian area. *** People on the meditation course were off on their own, meditating ten to twelve hours a day. The Beatles spent their time meditating, resting, writing songs, and attending the Maharishi's lectures, or talking with him on the roof of his bungalow. My days were free to meditate, relax, talk with Lew, and hang out with the Beatles, their partners, Mal, Mia and Prudence Farrow, Donovan, and Mike Love, usually in small groups at the table by the cliff. *** One afternoon, Donovan, Mal, John, Paul, George, Cynthia, Jane, Pattie, Pattie's sister Jennie, and I were sitting around chatting, talking about India, the Maharishi's teachings, and the beautiful ashram surroundings. Some were relieved to be in the lovely warmth, glad to be missing "the usual British winter." We talked briefly about meditation, in general agreeing that more than one voice would play in one's thoughts and the key was to simply go back to one's mantra. John said, "Not so easy, really. I often have music playing in me head." George seemed the most serious about meditation, followed by John. Paul seemed less serious, but he'd had several profound experiences, he said, enjoying the time he dropped away from

busy, worldly thoughts. Ringo was the least interested. John did say, though, that there was a friendly competition among the four of them to see who was really getting it best—the benefits of meditation. And Jane added that there was a competition among some of the meditators on the course as to

who could meditate longest. Apparently, a Swedish woman had gone the longest—forty-two hours. *** The ashram food was a major topic. It was good but bland to most of the palates around the table. Someone said that the Maharishi didn't want any of our meditations interrupted by upset stomachs from hot Indian spices. Mal quickly cracked everyone up with "Well, Ringo definitely won't have that problem!" One of Mal's responsibilities was buying and cooking eggs for Ringo, to go with his baked beans. Ringo had arrived in India with two suitcases: one filled with clothes and the other with cans of baked beans. Mal later told me that as a child, Ringo had been in and out of hospitals with stomach problems and always watched his food carefully when he traveled. George and John, already vegetarians when they arrived at the ashram, said they had no problems, but Paul was missing meat. *** Most everyone in the group was having the tailor outside the gate make clothes for themselves and as gifts for family and friends. During the day, the tailor took measurements; then each evening, he sat cross-legged on the ground in front of his hand-operated antique Singer sewing machine. He worked late into the night, a small circle of soft yellow light falling around his sewing machine from an old kerosene lamp next to his knee. And each night I drifted off into a dreamy sleep to the rhythm of the *click-clack, click-clack, click-clack.* *** The women were having tops and slips made, to wear under the colorful Indian saris they had bought, and some were also having a salwar kameez made—a very traditional woman's ensemble with a knee-length dress and pants. It's accentuated by a light scarf that hangs over both

PRECEDING PAGES: Paul; Ringo Starr; Pattie Boyd Harrison and George; Jennie Boyd and Jane Asher; OPPOSITE: Paul

shoulders and across the chest. The guys were having the tailor make Nehru jackets and kurta pajamas. ★★★ As we sat together, John, Paul, Ringo, and George exuded a decency and warmheartedness, without airs. As a couple, George and Pattie were self-contained and quiet. They seemed very much in love. Pattie's sister Jennie was young, about eighteen, always happy, and very beautiful—she was a model at the time. Ringo and

PRECEDING PAGES: John and Cynthia; OPPOSITE: Paul

Maureen had just had their second child together and seemed so comfortable, like an old married couple. ★★★ As I spent time with the Beatles, together or individually, Paul was the most overtly warm and friendly. Jane Asher was a lovely-hearted woman whose striking red hair framed a freckle-filled face of beauty and intelligence. Unlike the other Beatles and their partners, Jane and Paul were openly tactile and affectionate. They had been together for five years, and although Paul would say in the months after Rishikesh, after they had broken up, that he had not been in love with Jane, he also said that she had inspired some of his most beautiful love songs. John and Cynthia were different. They were both bright and friendly with strangers but distinctly distant and cool with each other. And they seemed to be sleeping in different quarters.

It was getting towards evening, the sky turning a lovely pale pink, and across the Ganges the sounds of Rishikesh were fading into dusk. A flight of forty or fifty beautiful emerald-green parrots landed dramatically in a nearby tree and glimmered like jewels in the evening light. Gradually, people got up to leave our gathering spot near the cliff's edge until, eventually, everyone left, except John and me. He was quiet, even a bit sullen, and I got the sense he wasn't happy. I asked him how long he

75

was staying. *** "We're all taking the Maharishi's course for three months, including Mal, and who knows after that." *** He looked at me very warmly, and smiled, asking, "What about you?" *** I thought for a moment, about my ex-girlfriend and the gift of meditation I'd already received, and wondered if he'd even care to hear about it all. What, with him being a Beatle and me being, like, an ordinary shmoe? The thought quickly passed and I realized that at that moment we were just two young guys, John twenty-seven and me twenty-four. *** I told him about my trip, the heartbreak, and how I felt about meditation. That I'd probably hang around for just a few more days. He picked up a glass of water, and after almost finishing it, said that meditation had been good for him, so far. After a moment he added, "Yeah, and love can be pretty tough on us, can't it?" *** We both sat quietly. It felt like a moment suspended in time. A lone hawk circled in the sky just above us and out over the river, so close we could see its talons. I looked at John and our eyes met, and he smiled and said, almost mischievously, "But then, eventually, you get another chance, don't you?" *** "For sure," I said. We were silent again, and after a while John said, "Off to write me music, then." We got up and walked together to the bungalow where he was staying. I continued on to my tent. *** It wasn't until I was back in Canada some months later that I read all about John and Yoko and realized that night he had been talking about himself.

THE INNER LIGHT

The next afternoon, as I finished meditating in Raghvendra's room, he said it was time for me to meet the Maharishi. I followed him out into the intense Indian sun and walked to the Maharishi's whitewashed bungalow. His house sat in a grove of trees at the edge of the cliff. We walked up the stone path, crossing the well-kept lawn between two small fountains, and past flowerbeds filled with yellow and orange marigolds. Several steps led up to a wide porch where we left our shoes. We entered a small, bright meeting room, separate from his private quarters in back. There was a low dais for the Maharishi and the floor was covered with white futons, where we were to sit. *** We sat cross-legged on the floor in front of the dais and waited until voices approached from outside. The door swung open, and after removing their shoes and sandals, John, Paul, Ringo, George, Mia, Cynthia, Pattie, Maureen, and Jane came in. *** "Hi, Paul, how are you?" asked Ringo. "Excellent," I said. "That's what happens here," said George, as everyone sat cross-legged around us. *** After a moment the Maharishi came in from his room and sat on the dais. He put his palms together and said "Namaste" with a giggle of joy. We returned the greeting. After some general words of welcome, hoping we were all getting along well, he asked George about the small black tape recorder he'd brought with him. "Is it a new song, George, or shall I recite the Vedas?" the Maharishi giggled again. "A new song," George answered. "I just recorded it in Bombay last month." *** George pressed the play button and sang along with his recorded voice and music. The Maharishi, rolling his prayer beads between his fingers, laughed approvingly. George smiled shyly like a new father as his song, "The Inner Light," filled the room.

OB-LA-DI

A couple of days later, I came out of my tent feeling blissful after meditating and walked up the hill to the back of the ashram, joining Paul, Jane, John, and several others at the table for tea. John greeted me playfully, saying, "You don't look so heartbroken, anymore." I smiled, as if we were sharing a secret. ✳✳✳ Later that afternoon, I heard guitars and the sound of Paul's and John's voices. They were sitting with Ringo among the potted plants on the steps of their bungalow. I got my camera, and, after taking a few pictures through the chainlink fence, I opened the gate and joined them. They were strumming their Martin acoustic guitars, singing fragments of songs, musically meandering through some of my favorites: "Michelle," "All You Need Is Love," "Norwegian Wood," "Eleanor Rigby," and others. ✳✳✳ Ringo was dressed in his favorite heavy, gold-brocade Nehru jacket and jeans, with his ever present black bag over his shoulder and his silver 16mm camera case nearby. He was calm, quiet, almost motionless. Of the four Beatles, he appeared the most serene, the most grounded, the most at ease with who he was. John and Paul wore white cotton kurta pajamas, the most comfortable clothes to wear in India, and leather sandals, or *chuppals*, in Hindi. And John, it seemed, never took off the leather talisman he wore around his neck. ✳✳✳ Having been photographed so often, and in the completely informal ashram setting, they paid no particular attention to the camera. They paused for a moment as I approached. John scratched the inside of his ear with a slightly faraway look in his eyes. I snapped a picture. Then Paul started strumming again and John joined in. Paul had a pad of paper sitting on the step beneath him, and he started to sing the words that he had scribbled down. It was the chorus to "Ob-La-Di Ob-La -Da." They repeated it over and over again, and when they stopped Paul looked at me with a twinkle in his eyes and said, "That's all there is so far. We've got the chorus but no words yet." ✳✳✳ John chuckled

Ringo, John and Paul

78

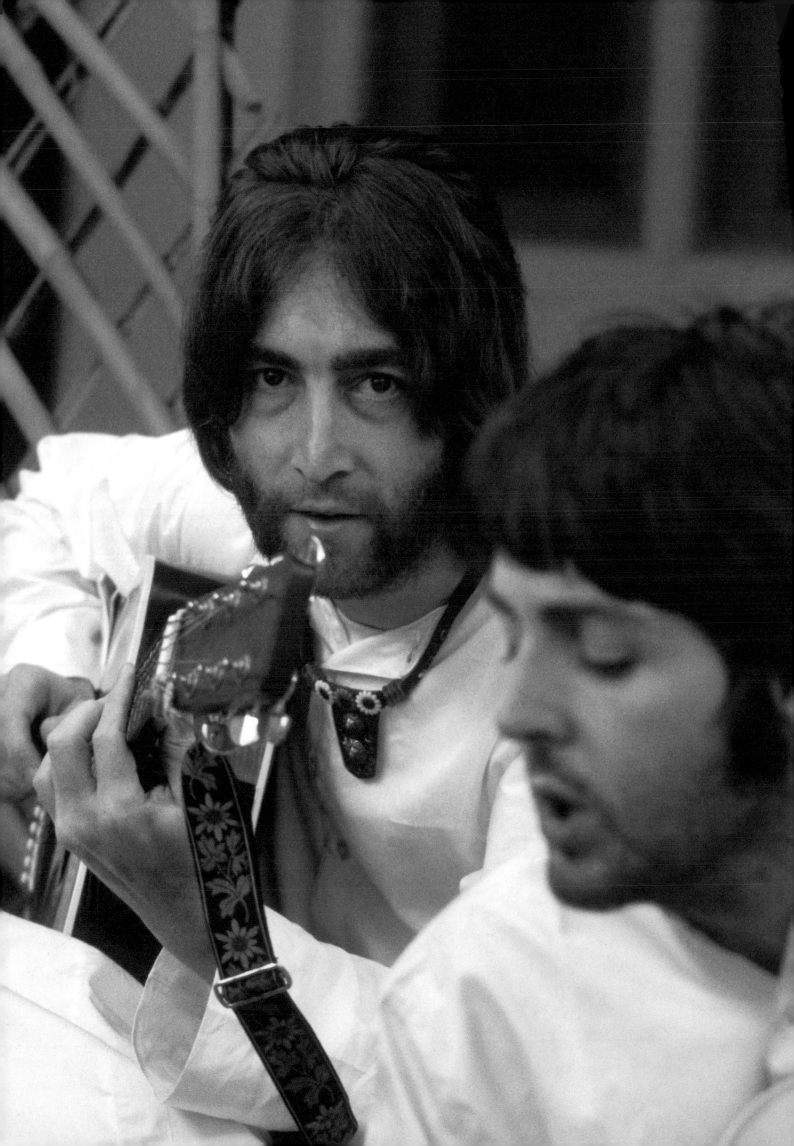

with pleasure at his new folk guitar picking technique he said Donovan had been teaching him. As they played, some of the men who worked at the ashram came over, listened for a while, then went back to their work. Some time later Ringo mentioned dinner was ready but as John got up, Paul started to sing and play "Ob-La-Di" again. John couldn't resist and fell in with him, playing and singing very upbeat. An old friend of Donovan's named Gypsy Dave and his Swedish girlfriend, Yvonne, wandered over and as the tempo picked up, Gypsy Dave clapped along, bringing in a rhythm line. By then the sun had dropped behind the hills. A gentle aroma of evening jasmine drifted over the grounds and a peacock shrilled off in the woods, and after a while we all headed off to eat.

DEAR PRUDENCE

Walking toward Raghvendra's quarters, I met Prudence and Mia Farrow out for a stroll. We greeted each other. Prudence stopped. Then Mia. "You're the fellow from the hotel in Delhi, aren't you? You came to our room." Prudence turned to her sister. "Mia, this is the guy who brought you that lovely big yellow mum." Mia brightened. "That was so good of you." Mia took my hand for a moment and smiled. "That was such a horrible day. We'd just arrived from New York, exhausted from the long flight, and then that press thing happened. But your generosity made a difference." I said I was glad, and after a few more pleasantries we parted. Mia and I had something in common that morning, and that was the reason we'd both come to Rishikesh. We had each gone to hear the Maharishi lecture, she in Boston, just a month before I had, in New Delhi, hoping to find a salve

PRECEDING PAGES: Ringo, John, and Paul; Paul; OPPOSITE: John and Paul

for the pain; searching for a new self-respect by going within, irrespective of the love of others. *** For those on the course, the Maharishi recommended twelve hours of daily meditation. Mia tried it but said she could do only several hours a day. Otherwise, she would read, sit by the Ganges, or walk down to the town below. One day she came back cuddling a stray puppy she had spontaneously adopted. Later, the Maharishi named him Arjuna, after a great warrior from the mythological Sanskrit epic *The Mahabharata*. Whenever I saw Mia after that, Arjuna would be in her arms. *** It was Prudence who had actually introduced Mia to meditation. At the ashram, Prudence immersed herself in meditation, med-itating such long

PRECEDING PAGES: John; OPPOSITE: John and Paul

hours that she didn't come out for her meals, having them sent in. After a while she stayed in her room around the clock. She was either blissed out or, as one of the Beatles later voiced, flipping out. Either way, it became a cause of concern and George, followed by John and Paul, tried to get her to come out. Prudence wouldn't even answer the door. I would be gone by then, but eventually, after three weeks of Prudence's staying in her room, John and Paul took their guitars and serenaded her through her locked door and drawn curtains, singing a little ditty John wrote for the occasion. According to Paul, it worked. The drapes moved slightly, and Prudence looked out. After a moment, a slight smile animated her face, and eventually she emerged. That little ditty was "Dear Prudence" and it became part of the Beatles' next album, the *White Album*. *** The Maharishi was star oriented. He seemed to fawn over the Beatles, Mia, Donovan, and Mike Love, but especially the Beatles and Mia. Late one afternoon, Mal and I were sitting together enjoying delicious cups of Indian tea, or *chai*. I

hadn't seen Mia in several days and wondered where she had gone. ✳✳✳ "Oh, she got fed up, mate," Mal said. "The Maharishi was sticking paper crowns on her head and trotting her out for so many photo snaps, she said it was just like Hollywood. She split and went on a tiger hunt." We both laughed. He added heartily, "He does love the publicity, doesn't he?" ✳✳✳ The Maharishi seemed sincere to me. He spoke in words and concepts that resonated within me. That he also was commercially oriented surprised me but, ultimately, it didn't bother me. What did bother me were the

The Maharishi Mahesh Yogi

exaggerations, or untruths, that organizationally surrounded the core gift of meditation. Teachers of TM at the ashram routinely said the Maharishi had rediscovered a powerful technique of meditation that had been lost for centuries. And several cautioned me never to tell my mantra to anyone else, telling me that my mantra was unique to me, and would lose its power if spoken to others. Neither of these claims were true. I was later told by another TM teacher that my mantra "ing," which was given to me by Raghvendra, was also given to thousands of people—as were other TM mantras.

WITHIN YOU, WITHOUT YOU

Another day I sat with the Beatles overlooking the Ganges. After tea, everyone left except George and me. Sitting alone with him I felt shy, awkward. George was quiet and intense but not unfriendly. He was then just a few days away from his twenty-fourth birthday. I asked him how long he had played the sitar, having loved it on their song "Norwegian Wood." ✳✳✳ "A little over two years," he answered. "It was when we made *Help*. We were filming and there was a sitar around. I was curious, but the first time I really listened to sitar music was off a Ravi Shankar album. Later, I was introduced to him in London and asked him to teach me. He agreed but it wasn't until I came here with Pattie last year, to Bombay, where Ravi lives, and studied with him for six months that I really got deeply into it. And into India and all it has to offer, spiritually and otherwise." ✳✳✳ A baby monkey dropped down onto the far end of our table from the thatched roof above, scampered four or five feet toward us, grabbed a crust of bread lying there, and chattered off, noisily. We both laughed at its apparent pleasure. "I'm going to play for a while. Would you like to listen?" George asked. ✳✳✳ We walked over to his bungalow and into a small meditation room, about eight feet by ten feet, with only a white futon on the floor, and his sitar. George sat cross-legged near the center of the room and I sat facing him a few feet away, my back resting against the wall. He nestled the large gourd at the base of the sitar against the sole of his left foot. Soft sunlight filtered through the slightly dusty window panes. Everything was glowing. I could smell the faint aroma of sandalwood incense from somewhere outside, and George closed his eyes and began to play. The sympathetic strings picked up the vibrations of the melody and the drone strings creating that unique, hypnotic sound of the sitar. The multilayered music, like a kaleidoscope of exquisite colors, filled the small room. My eyes closed and I drifted dreamily on the waves of sound. Time seemed to slow down. He played an Indian raga for fifteen or twenty minutes. As he finished, the musical reverberations slowly faded into silence and I felt a soft, delicious feeling of peace. ✳✳✳ When I opened my eyes, he was gently laying his sitar back down. The sunlight had shifted across the futons and there was a soothing aura in the room. ✳✳✳ In the relaxed converstaion that fol-

George

96

lowed, he told me that his wife, Pattie, had learned Transcendental Meditation first and then got him interested. I asked how it was for him. He responded, saying, "You can have everything in life. Like we're the Beatles, aren't we? We can have any-thing that money can buy. And all the fame we could dream of. And then what? It isn't love. It isn't health. It isn't peace inside." He paused, then continued, "Meditation and the Maharishi have helped make the inner life rich for me. I get higher than I ever did with drugs. The meditation buzz is incredible. It's simple, the vibration is on the astral plane, and it's my way of connecting with God." He gave me a dear, even loving smile, I thought. We sat a bit longer and then went out into the warm winter sun. ✳✳✳ The Beatles' interest in meditation and spirituality had begun several years before Rishikesh. George was influenced by the writings of the Indian scholar and sage Vivekananda and had been exploring the spiritual aspects of life for some time. As he found exciting books or passages, he would share them with John, Ringo, and Paul, who had their own interests in exploring such questions. ✳✳✳As they delved deeper into "spiritual" questions they found drugs less capable of helping them find the inner answers they were looking for. Earlier, smoking marijuana and hashish, and taking LSD for fun and for exploring consciousness, had brought some positive results, manifested in their songs. In time, though, drugs became somewhat of a dead end. I had experienced this as well. ✳✳✳On August 24, 1967, the Maharishi was giving an intro-ductory lecture at the Hilton Hotel in London and Pattie and George took the other Beatles along to hear him speak. Afterward, they went backstage for a private meeting. They were drawn to his message, and the Maharishi invited them to leave with him the next morning by train for a ten-day meditation retreat in Wales. But after only one day at the retreat, they learned of the death of their manager, Brian Epstein, and returned to London. When the Maharishi returned to the city they continued to study with him, and he invited them to Rishikesh for the three-month intensive meditation course. ★★★ It was a very exciting time for me, both in the sublime effects of my meditations and in hanging out with the Beatles. I meditated twice a day for a half hour each time, usually in the small meditation room where Raghvendra had first given me my mantra. I sat in a comfortable chair and closed my eyes. I relaxed by gently paying attention to my breathing. As I said my mantra, silently inside, and listened to it fade into silence, the outside world again receded. As I repeated my mantra, thoughts would intrude. Anything that was percolating inside: "This is dumb, I'll never get this right." "I wonder what's for lunch." "Jeez! Meeting the Beatles is such a neat trip." ★★★ Eventually, I would simply and gently cease the dialogue inside my head and replace it with my mantra. Over the days it became easier and easier to turn off the internal noise and self-criticism and repeat my mantra, following it to silence. In those exquisite, empty moments there was a true, deep peace within. ★★★ The day after George invited me to sit with him, the Maharishi organized a group photo of all those attending the course. He personally supervised the construction of raised benches for the meditators and a platform that he and the Beatles would sit on, front and center. When the four-tiered bleachers were all ready in the large clearing by the cliff, flower pots lining the front and the platform decorated with a swath of bright-red cotton fabric, two white-robed monks carried a small dais covered with an antelope skin onto the platform and placed it in front of a large painting of

99

Guru Dev, for the Maharishi to sit on. Everyone assembled, wearing a marvelous array of Indian clothes, highlighted by fresh garlands of orange yellow, and crimson marigolds. The Maharishi orchestrated where each and every individual was meant to sit. *** When all but the luminaries were seated,

PRECEDING PAGES: Mia Farrow

theMaharishi sat in the shade to wait while the photographer finished setting up. He'd had chairs placed in a circle in a nearby grove of trees where the Beatles, their partners, Jennie Boyd, and Mike Love sat together waiting for their time to be seated. Ringo was shooting his 16mm Beaulieu camera, while the Maharishi spoke about his hopes that meditation would spread to the youth of the world. The group listened as he outlined plans to set up a university in Switzerland where meditation would be taught and where research would be carried out on the "scientifically proven benefits of Transcendental Meditation." *** Some of the group seemed a bit bored, as if they had heard it all before, and Paul turned around to see what I was doing behind him as I took another photo. Mal was snapping some pictures of his own from the other side of the circle. Pattie was taking pictures too. George looked at me and smiled into my camera. Finally, the photographer was ready, and a relaxed atmosphere of celebration permeated the next half hour of official photo taking. *** The photographer was a rather stately looking man of about sixty, with a small shop in Rishikesh. He would duck under the large black cloth attached to the back of his old Thornton-Pickard, a wood-and-brass, 8x10 plate camera, to focus and check the framing. Then he would come out, stand beside the camera, and call out loudly, "Ready! Now everyone look happy!" And when certain this was so, he'd press the shutter-release cable he was holding in his right hand.

The Maharishi continued to direct the event, calling out to the photographer where the camera should next be placed and how many shots he wanted taken, and telling everyone, "Let everyone outside the ashram see how happy your meditations are making you!" While the photographer worked, people chatted and laughed, enjoying this festive moment like happy, excited school children having their class photo taken. *** When it was all over, we all went off for afternoon tea. Back at our digs before dinner, Lewis Lapham and I sat on the roof of the inquiries building and took a few official photos of our own. *** I was somewhat turned off by those meditators who worshipped the Maharishi. Paul, Jane, and I talked about him. They liked him and were enthused by his love for life. But they had a down-to-earth view of him. Jane was put off by his evasiveness. And the Beatles, Paul said, were upset by statements the Maharishi made when he was last in the United States. They felt he lost many American young people when he said that young men should obey the law and not evade the draft. *** "Any fool can make a law," Paul went on. "That doesn't mean it's right. The Maharishi doesn't know much about world affairs and we've been telling him about Vietnam, and what's happening there, so he'd understand why some of the young men won't fight. The Maharishi just laughs when he can't answer a question, and it alienates people. He really must learn to just say, 'I don't know,' when he does not. He'll be more respected for it." *** That evening, I heard that Mia had returned. Apparently, she'd traveled to Goa, met her brother, and was now back.

HURDY GURDY MAN

I first met Donovan Leitch sitting with Mal at the table by the cliff. He was twenty-one,

soft-spoken and friendly. He had an interesting face, long and rectangular, with a shy, almost internal smile. I asked him if he had just met the Beatles. He told me they had been good friends for a long time. Mal later told me that Donovan had written "Sunshine Superman" in admiration of them and that they often attended each others' concerts. In Rishikesh, Donovan

PRECEDING PAGES: Donovan; Jennie Boyd; OPPOSITE: Ringo and Maureen

was meditating, writing songs, and relaxing. Besides hanging out with the Beatles, he spent time with Gypsy Dave—about whom Donovan had written the song by the same name. While Donovan was at the ashram he wrote "Hurdy Gurdy Man" and "Jennifer Juniper," written for Jennie, Pattie's sister, as well as other songs and some poetry he later published in his book *Dry Songs and Scribbles*. ✳✳✳ That evening, as I was walking to the front gate, I met Donovan and Mia heading the other way. It was chilly and almost dark, and Donovan had a colorful blanket wrapped around his shoulders. A cigarette dangled from the corner of his mouth, which was a bit risqué since cigarettes were banned from the ashram. Mia was wrapped in a brown Kashmiri shawl and cuddling Arjuna, whose head nestled in her right hand. I took several pictures of the three of them. By then there was so little available light, I just set the camera speed as low as I could, opened up the f-stop as wide as it would go, and hoped something would show up on film.

Many years later while on a business trip to Los Angeles, I was standing at the Marina del Rey Budget car rental counter when I heard a familiar voice behind me. I turned to see Donovan coming in, his guitar case in hand. He was graying around the temples, yet the same modest, soft-spoken man I remembered from twenty-three years ago. I

PRECEDING PAGES: Ringo, Maureen, Jane, and Paul; Ringo, Maureen, Jane, Paul, and George with the Maharishi

Everyone assembled, wearing a marvelous array of Indian clothes, highlighted by fresh gar- lands of orange, yellow and crimson marigolds. The Maharishi orches- trated where each and every individual was meant to sit.

reintroduced myself and we chatted about Rishikesh. I asked him where he was headed. He smiled and told me he was driving to San Diego to play one of those sixties music revival concerts. "I'm amazed I'm still in demand, from time to time. I love playing live audiences, and the money is really quite good." We walked out, warmly shook hands, and drove off in opposite directions.

GOOD VIBRATIONS

Mike Love, lead singer of the Beach Boys, dressed like he'd come to India on safari, often wearing a white British colonial-style pith helmet, with long coats and accessories straight out of the wardrobe department of a Hollywood film studio. He wore a striking, long, royal-blue satin Nehru jacket for the Maharishi's official photo. Whatever he was wearing, Mike seemed to dress for effect. He seemed out of place at the ashram. He was cordial in an aloof, star kind of manner in stark contrast to John, Paul, George, and

PRECEDING PAGES: Ringo, Maureen, Jane, Paul, George, Pattie, and Cynthia with the Maharishi; OPPOSITE: George and Pattie

Ringo, who had no airs at all. Mike was known as the man to see if you needed something. He had stocked up on various provisions unavailable in the area, and apparently traveled down to Delhi and back to restock his ad hoc ashram store. He supplied the Beatles with rolls of Kodak still film, camera batteries, and one-hundred-foot rolls of movie film. It was also said, quietly, that chocolate bars, alcohol, and hashish might also be available.

***Ringo had lots of film for his 16mm camera. After teaching me how to use it, he asked if I'd shoot some footage of himself, the other Beatles, and the general goings-on for a film they were thinking of making on the Maharishi. A couple of days before I left the ashram for home, Ringo

117

124

handed me an unexposed roll of film, saying, "Here, Paul, shoot this for yourself and keep it, for the fun of it. Who knows, it might be worth some money one day." ✳✳✳ "I can't imagine why," I rejoined, and we laughed. ✳✳✳ Before I left, I filmed the Beatles. When I brought the roll home, I put it away some-where safe—and never saw it again.

NUMBER 9

Early one morning I found John sitting alone at the table by the cliff, writing. We both asked for chai, and when we had finished our tea and he had stopped writing, we got into a discussion about ego and altruism. I explained that at times I felt torn between these two opposing inclinations—to be constructive in society and to be self-serving. He laughed heartily.

"Good one, mate! Here's one of the great puz-zles in life: How to do good for

PRECEDING PAGES: Maureen, Jane, Paul, George, Pattie, Cynthia, and John with the Maharishi; George, Pattie, and Cynthia; the Maharishi, George, Pattie, Cynthia, John, Mal Evans, and Mike Love; OPPOSITE: Cynthia and John

others and at the same time for yourself. And where's the line between? I still have that in me head, too," he chuckled. "I asked the Maharishi about it the other day, and he said ego is not a bad thing. Actually, it's a good thing. The important thing, he said, was whether our ego manifestations result in good for others or in hurt for others. That's where you draw the line, mate. That's how you tell. Then we're doing good for others while we're doing good for ourselves." He paused and smiled. "You know, Paul, it's like the civil rights work you did. Someone said you were in the American South registering blacks for the vote a few years ago. Your civil rights work is a bloody good example of your ego doing something good for others and also feeling good about yourself at

the same time." *** "Yes, that's true," I responded. He tilted his head to the side and raised an eyebrow as if to say, "There you go," and went back to writing in his notebook. *** The days passed slowly in that sensuous way time unfolds when staying present in the moment. A few days later, I sat at the long table overlooking the

Ganges. I was writing a letter and Mal joined me. He told me he was going to Delhi the next day, that Maureen, Ringo's wife, was missing home and wanted to get back. "So I'm taking them to the airport and putting them on a plane." I had been thinking of heading home and asked if I could catch a lift. "Sure, mate," he answered. "We'll have two taxis. Gypsy Dave and Yvonne are going too, so you can ride with them." *** The next afternoon after lunch, I shoved my stuff in my backpack and swept out my tent. Then I meditated in the room where Raghvendra had initiated me two weeks earlier. Forty-five minutes later, refreshed, at peace, and looking forward to going home, I found Raghvendra in the garden and thanked him for his kindness. "Shukrya," I said in Hindi. "I hope we can meet again." "God willing," he answered. *** I went in search of John, Paul, and George and found them with Cynthia, Jane, and Pattie, sitting at the familiar spot overlooking the river where I'd first met all of them. We said our good-byes. As I started to leave, John said, "Send us some of your photos." Jane volunteered her number in London and said she would pass them along.

On the day of my departure, Lew left before noon to return to New York. We exchanged addresses, said good-bye, and promised to stay in touch. In the afternoon, Mal, Maureen, Ringo, Gypsy Dave, Yvonne, and I gathered to load our gear into the taxis that Mal had arranged. Maureen said she was

130

missing her children. Ringo teased her about the bugs she hated, and Mal teased Ringo about the food. And we all laughed. *** Then we began the six-hour drive south to New Delhi. Our tiny convoy dropped down from the heavily wooded foothills of the Himalayas, through towns with wonderful names like Muzaffarnagar and Modinagar, and out onto the plains leading to New Delhi. After a couple of hours driving through lush fields worked by turbaned farmers with hand hoes, we pulled into a gas station to fill up. We piled out of the cars and bought soft drinks, chocolate bars, and potato chips from an old Sikh with a wonderful long gray beard and a bright cherry-red turban tied loosely around his head, country style. He stood in his small, solitary stall by the side of the road, and above his head a rough-hewn, canary-yellow, hand-painted signboard proclaimed FANTA! Mal handed an orange drink through the car window to Maureen and joined Ringo and me on a bench. *** We talked awhile, finishing our sodas. The sun was setting, a large, orange ball on the horizon, its rays catching tiny ice crystals in the high wispy cirrocumulus clouds, lighting up the sky in a soft periwinkle blue. Exchanging warm good-byes, I shook hands with Ringo and Mal, then said good-bye to Maureen. *** Hours later, we entered the city. As the route to their hotel veered away from ours, they beeped their horn and we beeped back to say a final good-bye.

SEXY SADIE

After five and a half weeks at the ashram, Paul and Jane left for home. George and John stayed on—until the sexual issue exploded. In the tradition of Hindu holy men, the Maharishi professed to be celibate. Perhaps he was not. Whatever might or might not have happened, the Maharishi knows,

131

and the nurse from California, there for the meditation course, with whom the Maharishi is supposed to have had sex, knows. And, I believe, the Beatles know.   Mal later told me, "The Maharishi came on to one of the young women meditators, sexually. The evening John and George heard about it they stayed up all night, arguing over whether it could be true or not. They talked to the nurse from California, and they talked to others. When morning came, John and George went to confront

the Maharishi. John was livid. George was shocked and disbelieving. The meeting wasn't long. John said the Maharishi didn't take it seriously. He was evasive, and didn't respond directly." Mal continued, recounting that John clearly took it as a nondenial admission of culpability on the part of the Maharishi. George was not sure. They stormed out of the Maharishi's bungalow into the bright morning sunlight, went straight to their quarters, and told Mal, Cynthia, and Pattie to get their stuff packed, they were leaving immediately. They packed up, organized taxis, and quickly left.   At their hotel in New Delhi before flying home, they all talked over the situation. They knew the press would inevitably ask why they had left the ashram prematurely. They decided, Paul and Ringo later concurring, that they would say nothing of what had transpired between them and the Maharishi. When they landed at Heathrow Airport outside London, the press swarmed around George and John. Questions flew. "John, do you think the Maharishi is on the level?" a reporter yelled, to which John quipped back, "I don't know what level he's on." Though George added, "He's on the level." It has been variously written that the Beatles decided to say nothing because they didn't want to appear to have been taken for fools by the

138

Maharishi, or because they didn't want to invite lawsuits from him and his organization. John wrote a bitter song, apparently just before he left the ashram, which was originally titled "Maharishi" but for libel reasons the Beatles later changed the title. When it was released on the *White Album*, it was called "Sexy Sadie." John's anger, and acid assessment, comes through clearly. John gave up meditation, saying it was a waste of time. Years later he said, "There is no guru. You have to believe in yourself. You've got to get down to your own God in your own temple. It's all down to you, mate."

THE END

140

Some months later, I passed through London and called Jane Asher. We met for a half hour in a cozy tea shop in Kensington and reminisced. I gave her a set of four poster prints, one for each of the Beatles. "I'll pass them on," she said, as we shook hands on Kensington Road. I hailed a taxi and headed for Soho. Bob Baylis, an old acquaintance from the National Film Board in Montreal, had invited me to see a new Beatles film, but he wouldn't tell me what it was. I arrived at George Martin's Look-Listen Productions. Bob led the way into a small screening room and introduced me to picture editor Pete Hearn and animator Peter Sander. As we settled into large black leather swivel chairs, there was a feeling of excitement at the very first screening of the first "fully timed answer print" to come out of the film lab only one hour earlier. As the opening music of *Yellow Submarine* started, someone lit up a joint and we slowly passed it around. By the end of the film, the four of us were joyfully singing the last song, "All Together Now," along with the Beatles, with great gusto. The Beatles' time at the ashram was unusually productive. In all, they wrote nearly forty songs in

Rishikesh, including all thirty songs on their double *White Album* and much of *Abbey Road*. Most weren't specific to their time there, but along with "Dear Prudence," the songs "Long, Long, Long," "Yer Blues," "Sexy Sadie," "I'm So Tired," "Blackbird," and "Mother Nature's Son" came directly out of their ashram experiences. As did "The Continuing Story of Bungalow Bill," which tells of a very strange young man who came to the ashram, while I was there, from California with his equally odd mother. I was told that the mother was rich and important in the Maharishi's American organization and it was evident by the way the Maharishi treated her. At any rate, they arrived with numerous trunks of clothes and after the son meditated for a number of days he got bored, went off to shoot himself some tigers, and then came back to continue meditating. ★★★ Rishikesh was the last trip the Beatles took together. On November 22, 1968, within eight months of returning to England, the spectacular *White Album* came out. They did two more albums together, *Abbey Road* and *Let It Be*. On January 30, 1969, they did their final live performance together as the Beatles, for the film *Let It Be*, an impromptu mini-concert performed on the roof of their Apple office building in Soho, to the surprise and delight of passing pedestrians. It was less than a year since they had returned from India. ★★★ I had gotten what I came for from the Maharishi and in particular from Raghvendra. Before I left the ashram on January 28, 2000, I asked after Raghvendra. They said they didn't know where he was. Raghvendra was a profoundly kind, gentle, decent, loving man. It's said on the Internet that he was drummed out of the Maharishi's organization because he knew what happened at Rishikesh and he spoke out against the Maharishi's behavior. Apparently, it broke his heart.

It's said he cried for three days and that he now lives somewhere in south India. ✶✶✶ Today, I meditate using a method I find much more effective. I return deeply refreshed, connected with my Soul. And in this conscious place, all my worldly problems have a different feel and look. I approach my life from a place of love, rather than a place of fear—from a joy-based paradigm rather than one of struggle.

PLASTIC ONO

The last time I saw John was on September 13, 1969, at Varsity Stadium in Toronto. It was the world debut of the Plastic Ono Band, and they were part of a stellar rock and roll revival with Little Richard, Chuck Berry, Jerry Lee Lewis, Fats Domino, Bo Diddley, the Doors, and Alice Cooper. John was nervous as hell, throwing up before the concert, but as usual was fantastic on stage. With him were Yoko, Eric Clapton on lead guitar, Klaus Voorman on bass, and Alan White on drums. ✶✶✶ I can't remember where I was the day John Lennon was assassinated. I was too shocked and numb and depressed and angry. A few months before he was killed, John said, "If the Beatles or the sixties had a message, it was learn to swim. Period. And once you learn to swim, swim. You make your own dream. That's the Beatles' story, isn't it?" ✶✶✶ I'll always love the Beatles. Not just for their music, and the joy and love they transmitted, encouraged, and heralded, but also, as individuals I had the good fortune to meet and like and enjoy. When I say, "I'll always love the Beatles," I mean in a still, quiet way, as a deeply happy man who feels a flow of warmth in my heart when I hear their music, see their photos, or read their interviews. The Beatles were also four very human, ordinary guys who changed my life. Thank you—John, Paul, George, and Ringo.

✶✶✶

142

143

John said, "If the Beatles or the sixties had a message, it was learn to swim. Period. And once you learn to swim, swim. You make your own dream. That's the Beatles' story, isn't it?"

Paul Saltzman is a two-time Emmy Award-winning Toronto-based producer-director.
He began his film and television career in 1965 at
the Canadian Broadcasting Corporation before moving on to the National Film
Board of Canada. Currently the president of Sunrise Films
Limited—which he founded in 1973—Saltzman has produced or directed everything
from documentaries to family drama television series to feature films. He is a
member of the Director's Guild of Canada and the Academy of Canadian Cinema
and Television. *The Beatles in Rishikesh* is his first book.

Original prints from this book available at www.TheBeatlesinRishikesh.com